XAMonline, Inc., Cambridge, MA 02141
© 2011 by Sharon A. Wynne. (Text and illustrations)

Published 2011.
Printed in China by RR Donnelley
1 2 3 4 5 6 7

Lesson Ladder: an imprint of XAMonline, Inc.
25 First Street, Suite 106
Cambridge, MA 02141
Toll Free 1-800-301-4647
Fax: 1-617-583-5552
Email: info@xamonline.com
Web: www.xamonline.com

Text: Kristin Kroha
Cover and interior illustrations: Valerie Bouthyette

Library of Congress Catalog Card Number: (pending)

Kroha, Kristin.
    Sophie's Magic Underwear.

    32 pp., ill.
        1.   Title 2. Juvenile -- Fiction 3. Toilet Training - Juvenile Fiction

PZ7.K7643.S6745 2011   JFKro2011

ISBN: 978-0-9848657-0-3

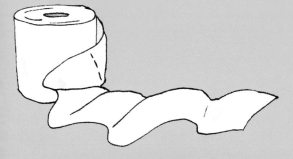

Sophie's Magic Underwear

Written by Kristin Kroha

Illustrations by Valerie Bouthyette

Hi my name is Sophie and **this** is Bunny.

We like to do everything together. It's kind of funny.

I'm a *BIG* girl now and can do *BIG* girl things.

I can put on my
BIG girl clothes…

…and Bunny can swing
on *BIG* kid swings.

UH OH! Excuse me! There's something I need to do!

Hurry, Hurry with me, Bunny! I need to go pee pee & poo poo!

Have *YOU* gone in the big girl potty before?

I will show *YOU* how. Bunny, shut the door!

I sit on the *BIG* girl potty after I pull down my pants.

And, I wait and wait....

Or, sometimes I do a bunny dance.

And then all of the sudden, I feel a very funny tickle...

And in the potty I hear a little trickly trickle.

Then I get up and wipe from front to back...

I also wash my hands and dry them on the towel rack.

But do *YOU* want to know a very special secret?

I'm about to tell you something magical…
(*SHHH!* Bunny, I hope you can keep it!)

What I do is take my wand...

And, I wave it around like a magical baton.

And, as I hold it
I take out a pair...

of my very special
big girl underwear.

With an

abracadabra

I put the underwear on…

and I don't have to go potty
in my pants all day long.

When I have to go, I just know.
I can feel something inside me about to flow.

So Bunny and I will hurry to the bathroom…

we go with a hop…

a skip…

and sometimes a *zoom!*

And, then there are days that I just can't hold it...

And, I go potty in my pants
before I make the toilet.

But, I know not to cry
or get upset…

It's okay to sometimes get my pants wet.

Because all I have to do is take out my wand
and put another pair of magical underwear on.

And guess what? YOU can do it too...

Because the real magic lies inside of YOU!